#MOMFAIL TALES

YOU'RE NOT ALONE - 40 MOM-COM STORIES FROM REAL MOTHERS
TO REMIND YOU ALL MOTHERS HAVE HAD THOSE DAYS

TM & Copyright© 2020 by Your Quirky Aunt
ALL RIGHTS RESERVED.

Published in the United States. By purchase of this book, you have been licensed one copy for personal use only. No part of this work may be reproduced, redistributed, or used in any form or by any means without prior written permission of the publisher and copyright owner.

Dedicated to every mom out there.
And wine, thank goodness for wine!

#MOMFAILS

Has your kid ever made you speechless? Like, what the F***?! Did you really just say that, speechless?

Every thought ran through your mind, but nothing would leave your mouth. Yeah, we've all been there. REALLY. We have.

To make you feel better about your own parenting fails, we have collected over 40 hilarious stories from REAL moms all over the U.S.A. and are ready to share the laughs.

Grab your wine & keep reading... But you might want to keep some of these moms in your prayers y'all!

Disclosure: These are real stories from real moms. These stories have been professionally edited and due to privacy, some names have been changed.

THE PROUD MOTHER OF A HOOKER

Like always, we were running late. A friend of mine was throwing a birthday party and my kids were doing that annoying thing where they exist.

I was so busy trying to pack presents, food and drinks into the car that I didn't realize what my daughter was wearing, until it was too late. Like every pre-teen known to mother, she started arguing with me, protesting that other mothers let their daughters dress like that.

I really wasn't in the mood and was about to tell her if she doesn't change right away, she could go find another mother. Of course I didn't say that - I said something stupider.

I told her she looked like a *"street walker"* which she didn't understand, but her younger brother was happy enough to tell her it meant she was a hooker! Remind me to remove his Fortnite access for a month!

Eventually, my daughter changed and we finally made it to the party, where my friend was waiting to help unload the car. When my friend asked why we were so late, my son chimed in for me and said, *"We were waiting for the hooker!"*

Remind me to also remove my son's access to food and water for the next month!

- SHARON

I used to have functioning brain cells, but I traded them in for children.

MY SON IS AN "ALCOHOLIC"

My son was graduating from kindergarten which was an excuse for us to throw a little party for him. When you have kids, you will use any excuse to have fun! Everybody came down including the grandparents, aunty and uncle and the house was packed with food and presents.

My husband thought it'd be funny to get our son a bottle of *"wine"* - Wait before you call Child Protection Services, it was just Welch's Sparkling Grape Juice!

My sister in law was on a diet and when my son attempted to pour her a glass of *"red"*, she declined as she was trying to avoid sugar. My son, not understanding this, looked at her with the cutest annoyed face and said -

"Oh, come on! It's not gonna get ya drunk!"

I don't think any of us have ever laughed SO hard!

- RAVEN

I am not an early bird or a night owl, I am some form of permanently exhausted pigeon.

DOES ANYBODY WANT TO BUY A KID?

My youngest son got lost at the grocery store. He's only seven but sometimes I bring him with me so he can trash the store instead of my lovely house.

I looked away for a few seconds and, like a typical child, he chose that moment to run off and get lost. Immediately, my mom instincts kicked in and I raced around the store looking for him, never having been so happy to have run track in high school.

Suddenly, I heard a voice over the speaker saying that he was at the front by customer services. I thought, THANK GOD... until I heard this little brat's voice chime in...

"*I'll only know it's you if you have a whole bunch of candy with you!*"

I was so relieved to hear his voice that I did get him *some* of the candy he wanted... plus some punishment when we got home!

Balance, right?

- CARRIE

The quickest way for a parent to get a child's attention is to sit down and look comfortable.

BE QUIET & EAT YOUR CORONAVIRUS FOOD

Like any rational person, the Coronavirus is making me act irrationally.

Just to be safe and prepared, I went to the store and stocked up on non-perishable foods for my family. I've got little kids so a good chunk of this was snacks and maybe... perhaps... totally snacks for their father and I, too.

My 8-year old daughter is pretty switched on and asked if it was because of the Coronavirus. I told her yes and these snacks were only to be eaten in an emergency, nothing else.

Their school was closed on Friday, but I had to work, meaning their babysitter dropped them off to me while I was at work. As they were eating their snacks, my daughter noticed my son had snacks from the Coronavirus stash and loudly shouted -

"Why does Ryder have the Coronavirus food?! Why is it in his lunch box?!"

Let's just say after this, my co-workers suddenly started wearing face masks to work, but that's completely unrelated, right?!

– EMMALINE

Motherhood is an experiment on how long your body can function without adequate sleep or nourishment, and fueled only on adrenaline, caffeine, and baby smiles.

LIFE IS LIKE A BOX OF CHOCOLATES

Sweets are life and you can't change my mind about that.

That being said, I had been doing my best to minimize sugar and eat less sweets. I even encouraged my husband to stop me from making last-minute grabs in the candy aisle.

My two boys, always in tow, often heard my husband trying to talk me down from buying any more candy. I felt that them hearing my struggle and seeing the outcome of me not getting what I wanted was a good lesson, never knowing it would soon come back to haunt me.

One day, I was in the check-out lane with my 4-year-old. I didn't notice the woman behind us reaching for candy bars – but he sure did. He put a calming, tiny-human sized hand on her wrist and said, *"Be honest with yourself, you don't need that chocolate do you?"*

It was one of those moments where you don't know whether to laugh or put your child up for adoption. Luckily, the woman laughed it off and said *"you're probably right little man."*

- MACEY

Not all who wander are lost.
Some are just moms.
In Target.
Hiding from their children.

LEECH HIM ALONE!

Who knew that watching *The African Queen* could save my son's life... Let me explain.

When my oldest son was about 5-years-old, we lived in a house with a creek near it. My son was playing down at the creek one sunny afternoon when he "fell in" and came home soaking wet. I freaked out and started tearing his wet clothes off him, and that's when I saw them.

Horrible, moving squiggly lines all up and down his body – LEECHES that were gorging on my son! Being little and not understanding he said, *"Look mom, I got little caterpillars stuck all over me!"* How do you tell your son that he's actually being eaten... well drank, alive?!

Luckily, I had learnt from Katherine Hepburn's character in *The African Queen* that you could use salt to get them off. Just as I was dousing my son in salt, my husband walked in, took one good look at us and walked back out the door. Later he told me he sat in the car for like an hour and laughed so hard he started crying.

- IRIS

Silence is golden.
Unless you have kids.
Then silence is suspicious.

THE GRANDMONSTER

When I was 16-years-old and a bratty teenager, I thought my mom was a monster... I never thought my little son would, too!

My mother loves her wigs, it's kind of her thing. I don't know whether she just likes looking different or considers it fashion. One day, she came to visit the family rocking one of her new wigs, and my son looked at her and immediately got scared.

"ITS A MONSTER!!!", he screamed as he ran to me.

Trying to hold in my laughter I explained that it was just his grandmother, but he was adamant it was a monster with hair!

Kids, you never know what they'll say!

- CHRISTEN

Some days, I'm rocking motherhood.
Other days, I'm managing snack negotiations with a band of drunken monkeys.

MIRROR, MIRROR, ON THE WALL, WHO HAS THE MOST COOTIES OF THEM ALL?

Kids have no concept of "mommy-and-daddy time." And if they do, they don't care.

One night, I was laying in bed with my partner; trying to remember that we were actually functioning, sexual beings before these tiny humans invaded. When from nowhere, my son burst into the room (because knocking is not a thing for kids) and pushes us apart!

He started teasing us saying, "*Eww nasty, you're both kissing! Mommy you've got cooties!*"

I wanted to say something like, "*Yes, and I want your dad to touch them*", but that really wasn't appropriate.

We ushered him back out to his room and had to accept that the moment was now dead. *sigh*

Next thing I know, I was walking past my son's room and I caught him making out with... his mirror! I thought, this is probably better than what I may catch him doing in a few years and just walked off laughing!

– DIAMOND

I hate it when everyone thinks I'm going to make dinner just because I'M the Mom.

I RAISED A (HOT DOG) JUNKIE

I don't know exactly what it is about hot dogs, but my 6-year-old can happily eat them for breakfast, lunch and dinner!

There was a time we were getting ready to go on a week long Carribean cruise, and everybody was crazy excited! When we boarded and got settled into the cabin, I suddenly noticed my 6-year-old walking around with a big smile on her face and chewing on a hot dog. When I asked her where she got it from she proudly revealed, *"I made a hot dog for every day on the cruise!"*

Ignoring the fact that my baby was now a stealthy hot dog smuggler, I reminded her there would be hot dogs on the ship. She looked at me dumbfounded and said –

"I thought they were just gonna give us seafood the whole time! We're on a boat!"

I wonder what she thinks we will eat on an airplane...

– ANNA

A mother's love is unconditional.
Her temper is another subject.

YOU GOTTA BE KITTEN ME!

My child recently found out what sound a cat makes.

We always watch educational videos together and he was fascinated by cats and what they do, eat, play - the whole thing! Well, the next day I found him literally stalking our cat, to the point I found him in the litter box while she was in it peeing!

Another time, I found him rolling around licking himself, purring "Meow, meow", and saying *"Mommy, look! We are kitty cats! I'm giving you a lick."*

Actually... he was giving me a headache, but I had to remember that it's not long until he's 18 and out of the house licking a real pussy, so pick your battles. HA!

- KAYLA

When your "mom voice" is so loud that even your neighbors brush their teeth and get dressed.

YOU CAN'T SIT WITH US!

I didn't know sweating was a crime.

I work long hours so it's a rare occasion that I get to be home with my kids before they're in bed for the night. One day, I managed to get out early, hit the gym and then raced home to see if I could catch the little ones before bedtime. Yay, I did!

I was so excited to read a bedtime book with them and snuggle that I totally forgot about my post-workout shower. There I was, lying in bed with my tiny 3-year-old, reading a book and singing bedtime stories when he looks me dead in the eye and says -

"*Can you leave now, Mommy? I don't like your bad smell!*"

Wow...tough crowd. Do I say that every time I have to change his nappy?! Can I get a refund on this kid, please?!

- KRISTA

You know you're a mom when being alone in the car is exciting.

HER FACE IS HER FACE, HONEY

Kids are savages. If they think you're ugly, you're gonna know about it.

One day, I was at my OBGYN's office checking my baby's heart rate and making sure the pregnancy was running smoothly. There was a nice nurse outside of the room looking after my son, and just generally keeping him occupied while I was getting my check-up.

After the check-up I sat in the waiting area with my son, where he thought it'd be a good idea to loudly say, "*That nurse looked like a freak!*"

It was at this moment that I wanted the ground to open up and swallow me whole.

He's got that high-pitched baby voice so I knew everybody had heard him. I took it upon myself to tell him that wasn't very nice and he could hurt somebody's feelings by shouting things like that.

Not getting it, or for lack of better terms, just not caring, he responded with, "*I didn't say she was a freak, I just said she looked like a freak!*"

Thanks kid, that's the clarification the nurse was looking for.

– VIDYA

My nickname is "Mom" but my full name is "Mom Mom Mom Mom".

ARRRGH, ME PIRATES!

My girls LOVE Spongebob.

They may not always get the humor, which I love because some of it is definitely written for the adults watching with their children, but they do love to sing along to the theme song sung by the pirate and I kinda... maybe... sometimes... always join them!

We were at the park, and they saw a veteran who had sadly lost his eye and had a blazer on with some of his medals. Naturally, I thanked him for his service - I can't even imagine the horrors he must have been through.

The girls, however, went with, "*ARRRRGH!!!*", and started pretending to be pirates. I was not impressed in the slightest, more like mortified!

The veteran, on the other hand, simply laughed and joined in with them. It was a truly beautiful little moment.

- PATRICIA

I hope your Mother's Day is more pleasant than labor was.

DO AS I SAY, NOT AS I DO, PLEASE.

The twins are messy... like REALLY messy! It's bad enough having one toddler around, but having two means that the house can look like a (toy) bomb went off at any time of the day.

I've gotten the girls used to "tidy-up time", but sometimes they get lazy and start throwing toys into this big toy basket. So many times I've told them that we don't throw things, but as all parents know, telling kids something 10x is the equivalent of telling them once.

Anyway, my husband is an avid basketball fan and he, like many others, was very devastated when Kobe Bryant passed away.

The other night during bath time one of the twins forgot her little plastic skateboard, it's her favorite toy for bath time - who knows why, so my husband grabbed it from downstairs. He shouted, *"Kobe loops it up to Shaq to dunk it!"* and threw it up to me. Keeping up with the game, I caught it and dunked it into the bath with the girls.

That's when one of my twins looked at me and said, *"NO! We don't throw things, Mommy."*

Dumbfounded, I looked at my husband who at this point is convinced that the girls are going to be full-on comedians when they grow up, so he loves to laugh at them! Hard to be mad when they use your own words against you.

- AMANDA

I don't want to sleep like a baby.
I want to sleep like my husband!

STOP AND SMELL THE FARTS

We wanted to smell flowers, NOT farts.

My 2-year-old and I were grabbing a few things at the craft store for a silent auction his daycare was holding.

As we perused the floral aisle, an elderly woman next to us suddenly farted really loudly and immediately, ran away in embarrassment.

My son, refusing to let the woman off the hook, loudly shouted, *"Eww Mommy, I think that lady just shit her pants!"*

I was so embarrassed AND flustered at the thought of where my son picked up that language, but the thing is... it smelt like the little one was probably right.

– ERICKA

It's like no one in my family appreciates that I stayed up all night overthinking for them!

I'VE BEEN DRINKING...

When my daughters were 3-years-old they had no concept of being quiet or doing anything slowly. They wanted to completely skip the whole learning to walk stage, and fast forward straight to the running part... which resulted in constantly falling over as they were trying to walk faster than their balance could handle.

My husband always found this hilarious and would say to them, *"Awe, have you had too much rum, girls?"* He's an avid fan of rum as he has family from the Caribbean, so it was a small inside joke between us. Well it was... until one day our friends came to visit.

The girls were running all over the damn place, intoxicated on the sweets our friends had brought them, and before you knew it, boom – one of them fell over. As their mom I know when they're really hurt, toddlers can be indestructible, so I just shrugged it off but my friend bent down to pick up my daughter and said, *"Are you okay?"*

To which my daughter replied, *"Yeah, I had too much rum."*

My husband was beside himself, laughing uncontrollably while I had to awkwardly explain that no, we haven't been turning our children into baby alcoholics.

– KALLIE

Parent Tip:

Never, I mean, NEVER make eye contact with a child on the verge of falling asleep.

They will sense your delight and abort the mission immediately.

PROFANITY CONNOISSEUR

So, I've been told I have a love of profanity.

This is what happens when you grow up an army brat, my dad cursed like it was running out of style, and he had to get it in now before it was too late! Not to mention all of his friends were just the same - profanity connoisseurs by definition.

One day, I was driving the girls to the store when some complete tool just slammed on the brakes and I almost rear-ended him! I went into full mom-mode, my one mission is to keep these cute, little, destructive things that live in my house safe, and here is this idiot almost ruining that.

Before I could stop myself, I had already honked the horn and shouted, "*Are you fucking serious?!*" Remembering that I was supposed to be an angelic mommy, I calmed down, turned backward and saw the girls were still engrossed in their iPads - Thank God for Apple!

A few days later when it was bedtime, my husband pointed at the clock and said, "*Girls you know what time it is?*" To which one of the kids put on her angry face on and shouted -

"*Are you fucking serious?!*"

Needless to say, I had some explaining to do.

- HEATHER

There's no one way to be a perfect mother and a million ways to be a good one.

– Jill Churchill

HOW MUCH FOR YOUR MOM?

It was the worst time of the year for me — Two words, *spring cleaning*.

As a single mom, it can be difficult to keep clutter at bay, especially when you have four tiny humans who were sent by the devil to mess up your house.

I'd recently learned of an app called *Let It Go* where people could sell unwanted stuff at a discount, so I thought it was a perfect solution to my problems. My daughter, only 7 at the time, loved the idea and started trying to sell everything and anything.

And I mean ANYTHING.

When I woke up in the morning I was excited to see lots of messages, except it turns out they weren't about the junk, it was about — ME!

My daughter had taken the most horrendous picture of me while I was sleeping, and posted it up on the app. It gets better... she had posted me for FREE!

I at least thought I was worth a couple hundred, no?!

– KRISTIE

Biology is the least of what makes someone a mother.

– Oprah Winfrey

MOMMY BY DAY.
CAMGIRL BY NIGHT.

My husband and I make our own pornos. There, I said it!

It's not something we've always been into, but with kids, jobs and general life… It's easy for the bedroom life to take a hit. It was our way of spicing things up a bit.

It was my husband's idea (so I should have known it would be a bad one) to hide these movies in actual DVD cases.

You can pretty much see where this is going…

Our 12-year-old son, Jacob, his cousin and friends tried to watch *The Hangover 2* one night, but ended up seeing my husband hanging over me.

There's no smooth recovery from this type of thing, but it's probably a good thing our town has really good therapists.

– CRYSTAL

We can't all look good at the same time.
It's either me, the kids, or the house.

MONKEY SEE, MONKEY DO.

Like any other kid, my girls love to draw! Give them a few coloring books and a box of coloring pencils, and they will be preoccupied for ages!

I left the room for 2 minutes to use the bathroom. TWO FREAKING MINUTES!!!

When I got back, I found them drawing on our lovely couches! I very calmly, lost my shit. You know the kind where you talk through gritted teeth and remind yourself that they're just children, and not actually assholes?

I pulled out my best mommy-voice and let them know that they can't draw on anything, except the coloring books. Proceeding to ask them why they would draw on the couch, when one of my girls turned her coloring book to me and said, *"We wanted a flower."*

I looked closer and realized that in one of the coloring books there are kids playing around a couch that looked oddly like ours and it had a floral design. *sigh* I couldn't really fault them for just trying to have pretty couches, too.

Oh, and all it took was 30 minutes of scrubbing and quietly cursing as they napped, and the couch was back to pre-artistry conditions!

- ANONYMOUS

Acceptance, tolerance, bravery, compassion. These are the things my mom taught me.

– Lady Gaga

WHAT NOISE DOES MOMMY MAKE?

Even though she's only four, my daughter, Scarlett, is already the comedian of the family!

One day, she was playing the animal noise game with her Mamaw, who asks her things like, "*What noise does a cow make?*" Then my daughter would respond, "*Mooo!*" in her cute little baby voice.

Mamaw thought it'd be funny to change things up and ask my daughter, "What noise does Mommy make?" To which she proudly shouted, "*NOOOOOOOO!*"

With laughter, she continued and asked, "*And what noise does Daddy make?*" Scarlett replied, "*YEEEES!*"

I laughed, but made a mental note to remember that for when she's 16 and asks me to borrow the car.

– BARBARA

If evolution really works, how come mothers only have two hands?

– Milton Berle

HAIR MY GOD!

So, I lied to my kid... But that's normal, right?

My 8-year-old son, Christian, thought it'd be a good idea to miss the school bus – Meaning I ended up having to give him a lift.

We managed to get to school early and I chose a spot in the parking lot a long way from the entrance, so I could take care of something. And by something, I meant these pesky little whiskers that have plagued my chin every now and then since puberty.

Honestly, they're an act of terrorism bestowed upon me.

When my son asked why we were parked so far away, I told him it's because he's a big, strong, athletic boy who can easily handle the long walk. He was loving this and started reading a book while we waited for everybody.

At some point he looked up, saw what I was doing and cried out, *"Not in front of my school, Mom!"*

How lovely, this is what I get for those 11 hours in labor!

– DIANNE

It's not easy being a mother.

If it were easy, fathers would do it.

– Betty White

WALK A MILE IN MY ~~SHOES~~ PAWS

Dinnertime is a good opportunity for our family to talk, no phones allowed.

Somehow, the idea of "*walking in some else's shoes*" came up and it took a while to explain to the youngest what that meant. I wanted to say, "*If Daddy wore Mommy's shoes, he may know that giving birth and getting hit in the balls are two VERY different pains.*"

But my husband was giving me a look like he knew what I was thinking, so I kept it to myself.

Later that night as I was on my way to the kitchen, I heard shuffling and a small commotion, so I walked towards the noise and found...

...My youngest holding our cat and eating some of its (Thank God, all natural and non-harmful) cat food!

Needless to say, I had to re-explain what walking in somebody else's shoes really means.

— CARRY

All that I am,
I owe to my mother.
—Abraham Lincoln

MY SON HATES MY FACE.

The truth hurts. Even more so when it's from your own 4-year-old.

My son, Eli, has a thing for make-up, hair, dolls, etc., which his father is totally loving right now. *sarcasm alert*

To bribe my son into taking a nap (don't judge me, you all do it!), I lay down with him and pretended to close my eyes. I thought he would do the same, but instead he just watched me for awhile, then asked, "*Are you wearing makeup?*"

I just mumbled "*Yes*", so he could hurry up and sleep, but then he said, "*I like your face with make-up.*" Okay... this made me curious, so I proceeded to ask him, "*So, you don't like mommy's face without make-up?*"

He stopped cold and looked me dead in the eye, "*NO!*" Then rolled over to sleep.

I was tempted to make it his last sleep, but he's lucky I love him so much!

— ALICIA

MOMSTER:

What happens to mothers after they count the three...

BEING A 'KELLY CLARKSON FAN' IS A THING

It's nice to know that even kids, sometimes, have no idea what the hell kids are on about!

My sister and I have sons of similar age. When they were about 6-years-old, Kelly Clarkson was really popular. Okay, I'm lying, Kelly Clarkson was really popular WITH my husband and I. There, are you happy now?!

We used to play her songs all the time with our kids, to the point that they really got into her music and knew all her lyrics. One day, I was riding with my sister with our two sons in the back and this is literally how their conversation went...

My son: *"Do you like Kelly Clarkson?"*
Her son: *"Who's she?"*
My son: *"She sings, 'Because Of You'."*
Her son: *"Because of me?"*
My son: *"No. She sings her song, 'Because Of You'."*
Her son: *"...She sings it because of ME?!"*
My son: *sighs and changes the subject* *"Do you ever watch... 'So You Think You Can Dance?'"*
Her son: *"No, I don't think I can dance."*

My sister and I were laughing so hard we almost crashed!

– TRACY

Anyone can be called a mother, but it takes a special person to be called 'Mom'.

THE PLAYER IN DIAPERS

Turns out, I've raised a player!

I had taken my 2-year-old to the clinic for a physical, and while we were waiting he started playing with the toys the clinic had left out. It wasn't long before he was joined by this super sweet little girl, and their parents and I smiled while they played together.

While they were playing, they suddenly stopped to hug, making everything 10x cuter! Then, my son kissed the little girl on the LIPS! We all knew it was innocent, but I was surprised, as I didn't think he had ever seen that kind of behavior with my partner and I.

My son went back to playing, but the little girl wasn't having any of it – She needed more! She started chasing him around the room, while my son ran around shouting, *"No more!"*

His father would be proud.

– KIRAN

May your coffee be stronger than your toddler.

MY NAME IS MOM. NOT ASS WIPER.

I am my son's designated ass wiper.

When my son was three, I was training him how to use the potty, and there was a time he needed to do a #2 and rushed to the bathroom. He promptly took off his underwear and pants before jumping naked on the toilet because let's be honest, children are odd!

I gave him some privacy before I went back in to put his underwear and pants around his ankles, so when he'd finished we could just pull them right up.

Or so I thought.

As I was doing so, he shrugged and gave me a look I didn't know he even knew how to do then said,

"But Mommy, you didn't wipe my ass yet."

As I cleaned him up, and my unhelpful sister laughed her own ass off in the background, I explained that we only use the word *butt* or *buttocks*.

— MEREDITH

Your mother is your first friend, your best friend, your forever friend.

THEY DON'T REALLY LOVE YOU.

My twins are getting to that stage where they're starting to question their surroundings. One night at dinner, they asked their dad and I a million questions about how they got here and why they look the same.

They're starting to realize that being an identical twin is actually kind of rare.

We're not exactly sure how you explain to a 3-year-old the ins and outs of the reproductive system, so we just went with, "*Because we love you both twice as much!*" - It seemed to satisfy them, so we dodged that bullet... for now.

Well, their older cousins were around a few weeks later and we'd forgotten all about that conversation, but clearly they hadn't. When my husband went to check on them playing in the garden he said he heard them telling my sister's kids -

"*Yeah, we look like this because our mommy and daddy love us SO much! Your mommy and daddy don't really love you.*"

Bullet *almost* dodged.

- GLORIA

Parenting is like folding a fitted sheet, no one really knows how the hell to do it.

YOU LOOK RIDICULOUS!

My child is probably going to be a 'World Champion Public Speaker'... this is a thing, right?

She's always had a vocabulary that far surpassed any of her peers, and I would like to take this opportunity to claim mom points for it!

There was a time when we were getting ready for church and I thought it'd be fashionable to wear a fuzzy winter hat. I walked into the kitchen to show it off to my daughter while she was eating breakfast. Well, she took one look at me and said –

"Mom, you look ridiculous!"

Suddenly, I felt like I was back in high school and getting teased – by my own daughter no less! I took the hat off to save both of us the embarrassment and got ready for church.

About 30 minutes later, we're getting in the car when she turns to me and says –

"Mom, what does ridiculous mean?"

I just laughed.

– MINDY

To be honest, I'm just winging it.
Life. Motherhood. My eyeliner.
Everything.

RAPUNZEL

My hair grows fast – I'm talking *Usain Bolt* kind of fast.

Don't ask me why, but I've made a special pact with myself that whenever it grows down to my waist, I get it cut short and donate the rest.

It normally takes around 3 years to go from short, to waist, so my young daughter has never seen me without super long hair. When she saw me for the first time after it was cut, she was really shocked, but the little cutie took it really well.

Or so I thought...

The next day when she woke up and saw me, she looked at me annoyed and said –

"Mom! You're still wearing your haircut?!"

It may grow fast, but maybe not fast enough.

– MIA

When I say,
"I'm just going to the restroom,"
My kids hear,
"Family meeting, assemble in the bathroom NOW!"

BINKY IN ITALY

Every child has that "thing" that they can't live without! My 2-year-old is OBSESSED with a pacifier that has a cracked rubber nipple, that he lovingly calls *binky*.

My husband and I took him on a trip to Italy, where one of his favorite places was a restaurant that overlooked the Mali coast.

One night, he was staring out across the cliffside, when he randomly took the binky out of his mouth and threw it over the railing. Not understanding that pacifiers can't fly, he went into hysterics as he realized his binky wasn't coming back.

We tried to console him, but nothing we did worked! 15 minutes later, a waiter came over to us with a domed silver platter, and initially I thought it was rude - as it really wasn't the time for more food.

But when he lifted the top off - it was binky! All clean and (kinda) new!

Thank God for Italians, they know what's important in life.

- DIANNE

I don't know why my kids
don't like time-out.
I tried it and I loved it!

ONE POOP TO RULE THEM ALL!

My son is a poop assassin.

I took my 6-month-old with me to a therapy appointment, and while we were waiting, I suddenly heard a noise. I thought maybe he had burped or was wiggling around and the sound had come from that.

I was wrong...

5 minutes later, I was struggling to breathe and wondered how something so small and perfect could produce a smell that came from the pits of hell!

My therapist was so appalled, she said, "*Call me to schedule your next appointment,*" and ran out of the room!

Talk about embarrassment.

- JOAN

I realized when you look at your mother, you are looking at the purest love you will ever know.

– Mitch Albom

I AM A PROBLEM FOR MY SON.

My son, Jacob, has an irrepressible need to get answers to his questions, immediately.

It's an issue he's struggled with both at home and at school, so we decided to seek help from Dr. Grant.

Dr. Grant asked Jacob how life was at home and my son told him a story of when I'd asked him to bring down a blue pen. When he'd gone to look for it he couldn't find it, causing me to go upstairs and get it. Only the pen was black, not blue. My fault.

On the way home I felt horrible for having shouted at my son over something so silly. When I asked him how he felt about the visit with the doctor, he said -

"Good! I had a feeling you were the problem. Not me."

Ouch. Right in the mommy-feels.

- MORGAN

"It's spicy!"

Universal mom code for:
I don't want to share.

MY ASS HURTS

Children have a funny way of saying things. I'd taken my son to the beach and we were coming home for a shower, as I took off his bathing suit he looked at me with discomfort and said –

"*My ass hurts.*"

I didn't know whether to laugh or give him a spanking and a real reason for his ass to hurt! Where did he even learn how to say that?!

I thought (and hoped) it was just a slip, but over the next few months he kept sporadically telling us his ass hurt. We thought it was good parenting to ignore it, until he realized that this wasn't something children should say.

One day, he couldn't stop informing us and when I asked him to show me where it hurt, he turned and pointed to...

His knees! – Where his rash was. *facepalm*

This whole time he had been telling us the eczema on the back of his knees, that was causing a rash, was hurting him. He was just mispronouncing his words.

Sorry kiddo. Mommy and Daddy ignored your ass (rash).

– NAOMI

Give me a double shot of whatever my kids are on.

DRAMA PRINCESS

My 4-year-old loves to be a princess.

She watches all the films and as far as she is concerned, she's a princess dammit!

One afternoon after watching *Princess Bride*, she threw on her princess dress and ran outside to be a princess.

She asked me to be the "*bad guy*" and chase her, which like any other good parent, I did! Because my daughter is quite the actress in the making, she pretended to trip and went down to the ground, where she proceeded to act out fainting.

I thought it was all fun and games, until I saw my neighbor watching with an agitated expression on his face as I pretended to grab her dramatically.

Thanks for the concern - my daughter is just a drama princess!

- ANONYMOUS

My house isn't messy.
It's custom designed by
a toddler.

HOW'S THE POISON, DEAR?

Visiting my sister's family is always a great time. I take my kids to play with their cousins and they love walking the dogs in the morning through the vineyard.

For breakfast, my husband and I would take the kids to a local bakery to order their favorite – hot chocolate and muffins. We'd all huddle together talking and for a brief moment we could forget everything and anything.

I told my kids about why I love their father and how he always lets me have the first bite of whatever he ordered in a restaurant. It was a romantic thing he did.

Turns out, I was wrong all along.

My husband then turned to my kids and explained, *"I do that so I can make sure the food isn't poisoned."*

Chivalry is so dead.

– OLIVIA

Mothers are like glue.
Even when you can't see them,
they're still holding the
family together.

– Susan Gale

A FOUL SMELL

My son, Thomas, has a talent for projectile pooping.

When he was only 5-months-old, we were at Grandma's house showing him off and taking adorable pictures.

Out of nowhere, Thomas decided to poop so viciously that it ricocheted off his diaper and spayed up his back - it looked like he had some sort of poop-cape on!

The sink was too small and the bath was too big, which left us with only one option...

We had to wash him in a large turkey roasting pan.

As I washed him, Thomas kept looking up at me like, "*Am I a joke to you?!*"

Haven't used the pan since.

- MEY

The influence of a mother in the lives of her children is beyond calculation.

– James E. Faust

FALSE ALARM

My 5-year-old is a rule breaker. Shocking, I know.

We were at my oldest daughter's elementary school, where lately there has been a rise in pranksters pulling on the fire alarm. To combat this, the principal installed ink on the handles that would leave a stain on the puller's hands.

Well, while we were watching the school performance, my bored 5-year-old decided to take a wander, where she saw a fire alarm - You can pretty much guess what happened next.

She pulled on the alarm, stopping the play and releasing a man hunt for the culprit! My daughter runs back to me with purple ink all over her hands.

It wasn't long before the principal noticed and proceeded to start telling her off. In-between the telling off, my daughter raised her hand to cut the principal off and said -

"Why are you shouting at me? I can't even read."

Legend response. I think that's the only time I've ever rewarded bad behavior with ice cream!

- DEANNA

I put the "hood" in Motherhood.

APPARENTLY, I'M RAISING A PICK-POCKETER.

So, it turns out my son is a talented thief.

One day during the summer, I took my 5-year-old son to the shops because he wanted a slushie and I maybe... totally... did want one, too. Slushies are for ALL ages!

When the time came to pay, I realized, like an idiot, that I had forgotten my purse at home! It was an effort to go home and come back again, but luckily for me - my son is a thief.

I told my son about me forgetting my purse and he proudly took $5 out of his pocket and handed it to me. When I asked him where he'd gotten the money, he said he had taken it "very, very sl...ow...ly" out of his dad's pocket.

Hmm... I wonder what he would do in a jewelry store!

I'm kidding... kinda.

- ANONYMOUS

It's wine...
a.k.a. Mom Fuel.

FIND MY SON!

Only a parent will know how easy it is to lose a child.

It was a lazy summer day and I'd taken my four kids to the beach alone, as their father was working and they were destroying my house.

I stayed on the beach with my little princess, while my three older sons ran out to play in the water. My two eldest, in their teens, went deep into the sea so they could swim, and their younger brother stopped when he couldn't stand up anymore. At some point he tried to walk back to his sister and I, but got lost instead.

You will never know true fear, until you can't find your child.

It was like the entire beach stopped and together we joined a man hunt with the police.

After a short while, my two eldest sons found him next to a large group of people who looked rather angry.

It turns out my son had been taking things like a water gun, soccer ball, etc. from them as he thought they were the same items he'd left with us.

In his mind, those were clues on how to get back to us.
In my mind... well, I'd already lost it trying to find him!

- MARINA

Naptime is my happy hour!

HI, I'D LIKE TO INSURE THIS LINGERIE.

My daughter is never afraid to speak her mind.

She was in a class where the teacher was discussing what they wanted to do after school and somehow the topic of insurance came up.

A boy in the class spoke about how some of his favorite sports stars have their limbs insured and the teacher asked, "*Yes, have you heard of Lloyds of London?*"

This immediately riled up my daughter and she called out the teacher for being inappropriate, as she thought *Lloyds of London* was the British equivalent to *Frederick's of Hollywood*.

I thought I'd have to talk to my daughter about boys and protection... not lingerie and insurance!

- ASHLEY

Check out our other books!

We would LOVE for you to leave a review on Amazon!

www.ingramcontent.com/pod-product-compliance
Lightning Source LLC
Chambersburg PA
CBHW070207100426
42743CB00013B/3088